Sports Strategies

SOCCER STRATEGIES

BY DAVID J. CLARKE

SportsZone

An Imprint of Abdo Publishing
abdobooks.com

abdobooks.com

Published by Abdo Publishing, a division of ABDO, PO Box 398166, Minneapolis, Minnesota 55439.

Printed in the United States of America, North Mankato, Minnesota.
102023
012024

Cover Photo: Marc Atkins/Getty Images Sport/Getty Images
Interior Photos: Julian Finney/Getty Images Sport/Getty Images, 5; Matthew Ashton/AMA/Getty Images Sport/Getty Images, 6–7; Joe Prior/Visionhaus/Getty Images Sport/Getty Images, 9; STF/AFP/Getty Images, 10; Lluis Gene/AFP/Getty Images, 12; Paul White/AP Images, 15; ANP/Dutch Height/Gerrit from Cologne/Getty Images Sport/Getty Images, 16–17; Marcio Machado/Just Pictures/Sipa USA/AP Images, 19; Eric Alonso/Getty Images Sport/Getty Images, 20; Shutterstock Images, 23; Jonathan Moscrop/Getty Images Sport/Getty Images, 24–25; Alex Grimm/Bongarts/Getty Images, 26–27; Team 2 Sportphoto/ullstein bild/Getty Images, 29; Israel Lopez/AP Images, 30; Harry Langer/DeFodi Images/Getty Images, 32; Denis Doyle/Getty Images Sport/Getty Images, 35; Ian MacNicol/Getty Images Sport/Getty Images, 36–37; Markus Gilliar/GES Sportfoto/Getty Images Sport/Getty Images, 39; Michael Regan/Getty Images Sport/Getty Images, 40; Robbie Jay Barratt/AMA/Getty Images Sport/Getty Images, 43; Richard Sellers/PA Wire/PA Images/AP Images, 45

Editor: Steph Giedd
Series Designer: Joshua Olson

Library of Congress Control Number: 2023939420

Publisher's Cataloging-in-Publication Data

Names: Clarke, David J., author.
Title: Soccer strategies / by David J. Clarke
Description: Minneapolis, Minnesota: Abdo Publishing, 2024 | Series: Sports strategies | Includes online resources and index.
Identifiers: ISBN 9781098292478 (lib. bdg.) | ISBN 9798384910411 (ebook)
Subjects: LCSH: Sports teams--Juvenile literature. | Teamwork (Sports)--Juvenile literature. | Athletes--Training of--Juvenile literature. | Soccer--Juvenile literature.
Classification: DDC 796.01--dc23

TABLE OF CONTENTS

INTRODUCTION

The point of any soccer game is simple. Teams try to get the ball into the opponent's net in any way they can. But there are many ways to make that happen during a match.

Soccer strategy is constantly changing and evolving. One of the sport's earliest popular formations played with five forwards and only two dedicated defenders. Any manager who tried that now would struggle to find success. Formations changed over time, and the way managers utilized their players did too. All the while, different playing styles popped up in different parts of the world. While England was playing long passes in the 1950s, players in Brazil were learning how to perform with tricks and flair.

Today, highly skilled players come from all over the world. So do the managers who coach them on top club teams. They all blend to create styles of play and strategies. Some teams have a set strategy they play all the time. Others change things up depending on that day's opponent or even during a match. Coaches change plans to fit a certain situation, protect a lead, or mount a comeback. However they are used, soccer tactics present a fascinating on-field battle in every match.

There was an average of 53,191 fans in attendance at each game of the 2022 FIFA World Cup.

23
crypto.com

Chapter 1

The Possession Game

Manchester City was in trouble. The English powerhouse entered the final day of the 2021–22 Premier League season needing a win to clinch the title. But they found themselves down 2–0 to Aston Villa with 20 minutes left. Without a comeback from Manchester City, rival Liverpool could jump ahead of them in dramatic style.

Even though Manchester City was losing, it had dominated possession of the ball all game. The team only had to make it count on the scoreboard. Despite having the lead, the Aston Villa players were growing

Manchester City's İlkay Gündoğan, *left*, competes for the ball with an Aston Villa defender during a Premier League match in 2022.

increasingly tired chasing Manchester City all over the field. Finally, in the 76th minute, City winger Raheem Sterling fed midfielder İlkay Gündoğan for a close-range header. Gündoğan knocked it into the goal to cut Aston Villa's lead in half. Two minutes later, more patient passing set up left back Oleksandr Zinchenko on the left wing. He dribbled around two defenders, then rolled a pass to the edge of the penalty area. Midfielder Rodri stepped up and hit the ball with his first touch. He drove a low, accurate shot toward the corner of the net. It beat the lunging goalkeeper to tie the game.

In the 81st minute, Manchester City was back on the attack. A through ball into the Aston Villa box was kicked loose by a defender. City's superstar playmaker Kevin De Bruyne sprinted to it. In full stride, he rolled a pass to the back post. Gündoğan was waiting there to tap it in.

The 3–2 comeback was thrilling for the home fans at the team's Etihad Stadium. But they weren't surprised. Manchester City never seemed to be truly out of a game, because the team always had the ball. The stat sheet showed that City had held the ball for 71 percent of the game against Aston Villa. As a result, City took 24 shots to Aston Villa's four. It was enough to seal Manchester City's fourth Premier League title in five years. For such a powerful team, the formula was simple—dominate the possession to dominate the game.

Midfielder Kevin De Bruyne of Manchester City races ahead to make a play against Aston Villa.

TOTAL FOOTBALL

Legendary player Johan Cruyff once said, "Without the ball, you can't win. If we have the ball, they can't score." Cruyff rose

Johan Cruyff (14) of the Netherlands dribbles past Argentina's goalkeeper for a goal in 1974.

to fame while playing for Ajax of Amsterdam and the Netherlands national team in the 1960s and 1970s. Those teams transformed how the game was played.

In the past, soccer was a sport of long passes. Defenders usually tried to get the ball up the field as quickly as possible to the more skilled forwards. From there the forwards tried to break through the other team's defense. If the attack didn't work, they would patiently wait for their defense to win it back again.

A Fluid Situation

Players who teamed with Johan Cruyff to play Total Football had to be flexible. Since the players switched places often, no one was tied to one position. The team's forwards were skilled defenders, and the defensive players would often move up to play attacking spots. Using that system, Ajax won the European Cup, which is now known as the Champions League, every year from 1971 to 1973.

Those Ajax teams helped change that style of play. Cruyff and his teammates weaved all over the field. They tried to keep the ball as much as possible, working it up the field more slowly using shorter, controlled passes. This style came to be called Total Football.

Today many of the best teams in the world play some version of that style. Manchester City is one of them. During the 2021–22 season, the Citizens played 38 Premier League games. They controlled the ball more than the other team in every game. A team that controls possession 60 percent of the time in a game is more likely to win the game. Manchester City had at least 70 percent possession 19 times in 2021–22. It had a record of 15 wins, three draws, and only one loss in those games.

Barcelona coach Pep Guardiola, *right*, talks strategy with his star player Lionel Messi, *left*, during a 2010 match.

TIKI-TAKA

Manchester City's manager is Pep Guardiola. The Spaniard is thought to be one of the best managers in the sport going back to his first coaching job at Barcelona starting in 2008. His teams were known for their short, quick passing style. It was even given a name—*tiki-taka,* which comes from a Spanish phrase that roughly translates as "touch touch." During his four years at Barcelona, Guardiola's teams won three titles in La Liga, Spain's best professional league. They also won the European Champions League twice.

Many of Guardiola's top players also played for the Spanish national team. That included key midfielders Xavi and Andrés Iniesta. In 2010 Spain used that tiki-taka style of play to win the World Cup for the first time. Spain had won the European Championships in 2008 and again in 2012. The two Barcelona stars, Xavi and Iniesta, with their skilled passing, led the way to all three titles.

THE FATIGUE EFFECT

Late in a match in November 2018 against rival Manchester United, Manchester City picked up possession near the halfway line. Over the next three minutes, every player on the team except the goalkeeper touched the ball at least once. City players patiently moved the ball backward and forward, and from sideline to sideline, looking for the right opening.

By the time it was over, Manchester City had completed 44 straight passes. The last one was a cross from winger Bernardo Silva to Gündoğan, who was all alone in the middle of the penalty area. Gündoğan scored easily to finish off a 3–1 win.

One of the reasons Gündoğan found himself so open was that the Manchester United defenders were exhausted. For that entire stretch of play, they were chasing City players all over the field, trying to win the ball back. That's one of the biggest reasons why teams like to play possession soccer. It's challenging to defend. And over the course of a 90-minute game, it can tire the other team out.

Possession soccer doesn't work for everyone. A team must have the right players to keep the ball. And talented players cost a lot of money. At Barcelona, Guardiola leaned on his high-dollar players such as Xavi, Iniesta, and superstar Lionel Messi. At Manchester City, Silva, Gündoğan, and De Bruyne are often the most talented and highest-paid players on the field.

Everyone who suits up for Manchester City must be able to control the ball, though. Even the team's goalkeeper, Ederson, is considered an excellent passer. That's why the team became consistently dominant in England after Guardiola took over in 2016. Since they have the ball so often, it's only a matter of time before good things happen.

Xavi is an eight-time La Liga champion and a four-time Champions League champion.

CHAPTER 2

THE HIGH PRESS

The 2022 European Women's Champions League final was a dream matchup for fans. The game featured Olympique Lyonnais (Lyon) of France against Barcelona. Lyon was the most successful team in the history of the women's European club game. It had won seven Champions League titles since 2011. That included five straight between 2016 and 2020. But Barcelona was a rising power. The club, from the Catalonia region of Spain, was the defending champion and boasted superstars such as Spain's Alexia Putellas and Swedish playmaker Fridolina Rolfö.

Lyon star Amandine Henry readies herself to shoot in the European Women's Champions League final.

SWORD
VENUE
adidas

From the opening minutes of the game, Lyon went on the attack. All over the field, the French champions battled for every ball. Barcelona was used to seeing opponents sit back, hoping to contain its powerful offensive game. Lyon did the exact opposite.

Just six minutes into the game, the strategy paid off. Lyon's Ada Hegerberg had the ball on the left wing. She tried to play a pass back to teammate Amandine Henry, but she didn't get enough on it. The ball was up for grabs.

Henry had two choices. She could back off and make sure she didn't leave a space open behind her, or she could challenge for the ball. Henry went sliding after it. With a heavy tackle, she knocked it away just before Putellas got there. Then Henry got back to her feet and collected the loose ball. She was 30 yards from the goal but wide open. The midfielder ripped a strong, curling shot just inside the far post.

It was an incredible goal that sent Lyon on its way to a 3–1 victory. And while the stunned fans who saw it will always remember the shot, that was just half of the play. It was the pressure that made it possible.

UNDER PRESSURE

Scoring in soccer is difficult. Finding a way to beat 10 outfield defenders with enough space for a shot is a tall task. Even the

Lyon forward Ada Hegerberg led the top French women's league in assists during the 2018–19 season.

best teams are more likely to turn the ball over without ever getting an attempt on goal.

Once a team does turn the ball over, it must regroup and get ready to defend. To do this, some teams immediately drop back. They hunker in close to their own goal and make

Added pressure from a defender can lead to mistakes from the offensive player.

sure there is no room for their opponent to move into the dangerous scoring areas. This is called a low block. Teams that do it rarely take chances in terms of winning the ball back. It's all about waiting for the other team to force an opportunity or make a mistake. A strategy called a mid block is the same thing, but the team engages the offense higher up the field toward the attacking goal.

Then there is a third option for teams who want to put the other team under more stress. When some teams lose the ball, they like to quickly get organized high up the field. By doing so, they can immediately make it tough for opponents to move the ball forward. At its best, this pressure can cause quick turnovers and lead to easy scoring chances. While some call this the high block, its more common name is the high press.

PRESSING FOR GLORY

The US Women's National Team used the high press effectively in its early years. Coach Anson Dorrance took the team to what is now considered the first Women's World Cup in 1991. There he unleashed three terrific forwards to pressure the team's opponents. Michelle Akers, Carin Jennings, and April Heinrichs made life miserable for opposing defenders. The United States outscored its opponents 25–5 over six matches to win the championship.

A LOT OF RUNNING

Not everyone can play the high press. It takes a certain style of player to make it work. Unlike the possession game, in which a team needs quality technical players to keep possession of the ball, the high press calls for a different type of player—one who is willing to run hard to win the ball back.

Since soccer is such a physically demanding game, many teams look for ways to conserve energy during a match. High-pressing teams do not. Players in this system run more than those in most other playing styles.

Pressing high can be risky, so players need to work together. For the system to work, every outfield player needs to push higher up the field, including defenders. That leaves a lot of space behind the back line. If any member of the pressing team's forward line or midfield group steps out of line, that allows the other team a way past the press. It can put the defenders under extreme pressure. This can also give the other team easy counterattacking opportunities. One of the things Lyon did so well against Barcelona was to stay organized.

PRESSING THE PRESSERS

Entering the 2022 Champions League final, it was Barcelona that had the reputation as the team that would press its opponents. Barcelona had done just that in the quarterfinals against rival Real Madrid. Barcelona's pressure over both matches in a two-legged playoff earned it a combined 8–3 win.

Lyon is known as an attacking team but not always a pressing team. Entering the match, many wondered how the club might play against a talented team like Barcelona. Lyon manager Sonia Bompastor decided it was best to throw Barcelona's strategy right back at the Spanish club.

Bompastor's forward line of Hegerberg, Melvine Malard, and Delphine Cascarino pressured Barcelona's defenders throughout the first half. They were backed up by the midfield

Lyon's Press

Each Lyon player, *X*, is accountable for an opposing player, *O*.

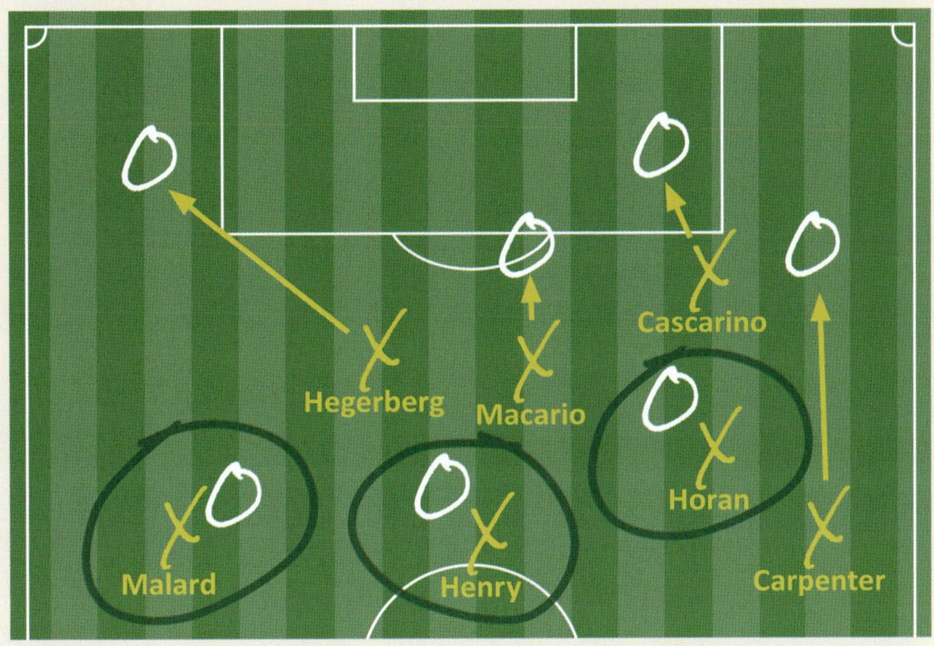

trio of Lindsey Horan, Catarina Macario, and Henry. That group shadowed Barcelona's midfield and didn't allow any clean passes forward.

Lyon's third goal was a terrific example of pressing. Cascarino caused a turnover on the right wing just outside the Barcelona penalty area. She slid a pass to Hegerberg, who tried to center a ball for Malard. The shot was blocked, but instantly all three forwards took up pressing positions again. A Barcelona defender tried to clear the ball from inside the six-yard box. But Malard blocked it and quickly flipped the ball back to Hegerberg. The Norwegian star had a clear lane across the goal to an open Macario in the six-yard box. The ball beat the disorganized Barcelona defense, and Macario tapped it in to make the score 3–0. It was the finishing touch on a perfect first-half performance. And Lyon pressed its way to an eighth European title.

Lyon celebrates its European Women's Champions League final win over Barcelona in 2022.

NNERS
S CHAMPIONS LEAGUE 2021/22
OLYMPIQUE LYONNAIS
OL

Chapter 3

The Counterattack

Bayern Munich's Franck Ribéry was looking for an opening. His team was down 2–0 in the first half of the 2014 European men's Champions League semifinals second leg to Real Madrid. The German team was pushing players forward, trying to get back in the game. But as Ribéry dribbled back and forth inside the Real Madrid penalty area, all he saw was a wall of the Spanish club's famous white shirts.

Ribéry finally decided to give up the ball by passing to a teammate at the top of the penalty area. Real Madrid's Gareth Bale

Bayern Munich's Franck Ribéry, *right*, and Gareth Bale of Real Madrid fight for possession during their semifinal match in the 2014 European men's Champions League.

adidas
7
RM

snuck in and made an interception. From that moment, Real Madrid's forward line raced upfield as if shot out of a cannon.

Bale played a simple pass to Ángel Di María, then took off up the middle of the field. Di María played a long ball for forward Karim Benzema, who was sprinting down the right wing. Benzema hit Bale in stride. Bale outraced a Bayern defender and was clear through to the goal. At the last second, he spotted Cristiano Ronaldo sprinting in on his left. Bale laid the ball in Ronaldo's path, and the Portuguese superstar hammered home a goal to make it 3–0.

From the time of Ribéry's ill-fated pass, it took just under 13 seconds for Real Madrid to go the length of the field and score. It was the kind of moment the club had made famous in previous seasons. Once Real Madrid's superstars got on the counterattack, almost no one could stop them.

SPEED AND PRECISION

Real Madrid plays in three big competitions every season. The team is always at or near the top of La Liga. Like all Spanish teams, Real also appears in the country's top cup competition, the Copa del Rey. And the club has been a regular contender in the Champions League every year since 1997–98.

However, entering the 2010–11 season, Real Madrid had not won any of those competitions for three years. For one of the

Real Madrid's star forward, Cristiano Ronaldo, scores against Bayern Munich in the 2014 Champions League semifinals to put his team up 3–0.

most successful club teams in soccer history, that was a long time. Luckily for Real Madrid, a new manager was on the way, and he had won everywhere he had been before.

José Mourinho of Portugal took over Real Madrid in 2010. He was a superstar in the soccer coaching world. Mourinho had won league titles with clubs in Portugal, England, and Italy. He'd also won the Champions League twice.

Mourinho instantly made Real Madrid a counterattacking force. Unlike teams that press high or hold the ball, teams that counterattack use a mixture of discipline, skill, and speed.

Real Madrid coach José Mourinho is lifted by his team in celebration of their Copa del Rey championship in 2011.

Counterattacking teams play a deep defensive line. That means they need to be patient and wait until the right moment to win the ball. Once they do, they must know immediately what to do with it. Defenders and midfielders get the ball up the field quickly to an open player. From there the attacking players strike before the opponents can get back in position.

A good counterattack can look chaotic, but in truth it is carefully planned on the practice field. Once a counterattacking team gets possession, the player with the ball immediately looks to pass to a player along one sideline to get the ball out of traffic. From there, the rest of the team's attacking players fill three channels. One player sprints up the middle. Two more fill in the lanes on the right and left wings. If those players outnumber the remaining defenders, the player with the ball suddenly has three options for the next pass. And the defenders don't know which players to focus on. After that it comes down to the skill and decision-making of the players bearing down on goal.

THE RIGHT TOOLS

A team can't counterattack unless it has speed up front. In Di María, Ronaldo, and Benzema, Mourinho had that. But he also had midfielders like Spaniard Xabi Alonso and Brazilian Kaká who could play perfect passes. On defense, where many counterattacks start, Sergio Ramos was great at playing accurate passes while under pressure.

Mourinho eventually left Real Madrid after the 2012–13 season. But his hard work in laying the foundation for the style of play remained. New manager Carlo Ancelotti had even more talent on the field. Bale, one of the fastest players in

Playing for the Croatian national team, Real Madrid midfielder Luke Modrić was awarded the 2018 FIFA World Cup Golden Ball as the tournament's best player.

the world, joined the team in September 2013. His speed was immediately on display in the 2014 Copa del Rey final against rival Barcelona. After picking up a pass on the left sideline in his own half, Bale tapped it forward and started a footrace with a Barcelona defender. Even though he was bumped off stride and veered several feet out of bounds at one point, Bale was still able to outrun his opponent and catch up with the ball. He sprinted into the box and scored the match-winning goal.

The talent and the managers continued to change at Real Madrid throughout the 2010s, but no one could stop their lightning-quick breaks. Croatian midfielder Luka Modrić became the player springing Ronaldo and Bale forward with his skillful long passes. After Bale and Ronaldo both left the club, Modrić started combining with young Brazilian superstar Vinicius Júnior. That duo led Real Madrid to its record 14th Champions League title in 2022.

BATTLE OF STYLES

Counterattacking can be an effective strategy to use against both teams that like to press and those that like to hold the ball. All it takes is one breakdown from the press or one wild pass, and the counterattacking team is off to the races. Mourinho was managing Real Madrid at the same time Pep Guardiola was using his possession style at Barcelona. Battles between the two heated rivals were always fascinating.

The final meeting between the two managers at those giant clubs came on April 21, 2012. Real Madrid held the top spot in La Liga's standings before the match started, and the season was nearly over. A victory could seal that year's title for the club. The match was tied 1–1 with under 20 minutes to go when Real defender Álvaro Arbeloa won the ball in the defensive half of the field. He quickly played it to Di María. The Argentine forward swung it wide to playmaker Mesut Özil. Ronaldo went streaking down the middle of the field. Özil laid a perfect pass into Ronaldo's path. Real Madrid's best player finished off the move with a powerful shot and goal. Three weeks later, Real Madrid ended the season as La Liga champions. The club had its unstoppable transition play to thank for it.

Big Numbers

Cristiano Ronaldo's goal against Barcelona in April 2012 was Real Madrid's 109th of the La Liga season, which set a new league record. Real Madrid played four more matches in the competition and finished the year with 121 goals over 38 games.

Real Madrid goalie Iker Casillas hoists the La Liga championship trophy with his team in 2012.

Chapter 4

Route One

With less than 18 minutes left in the 2022 men's World Cup quarterfinals, Argentina's Lionel Messi smashed home a penalty kick to put his country up 2–0 against the Netherlands. On the Netherlands' bench, veteran manager Louis van Gaal knew his team was in trouble. All match long, the Dutch had struggled to generate offense.

A few minutes later, van Gaal put in a substitute to try to mix things up. Striker Wout Weghorst entered the match in place of winger Memphis. The two players could not have been more different. Memphis is

Wout Weghorst celebrates after scoring during the 2022 men's World Cup in Qatar.

19

a 5-foot-9-inch speedster who can dribble around opponents. Weghorst isn't known for his excellent touch on the ball. But at 6 feet, 6 inches, he is a threat in the air. Instead of trying to play through Argentina, van Gaal was going to try to play over his opponents.

Immediately, the Netherlands started lobbing balls into Argentina's penalty area. With eight minutes left in normal time, Weghorst latched on to a cross from the right wing and headed it down into the center of the net to cut Argentina's lead in half.

Weghorst scored again in the final seconds of stoppage time to tie the match. Even though Argentina eventually won on penalty kicks, van Gaal's decision to play long-ball soccer had nearly sprung an amazing comeback. It was proof that sometimes the simplest of strategies can work wonders.

AN ENGLISH STYLE

Playing long balls is nothing new in soccer. For many of the sport's early years, it was the main strategy that all teams used: Get the ball up the field quickly and let forwards go to work. It had many names. Some simply called it long-ball soccer. Others called it "kick and run." The name that has stuck through the years, though, is "Route One" soccer. It's called that because long passes are the most direct way forward.

At 6 feet, 6 inches, Weghorst, *right*, is almost one foot taller than Lionel Messi, *left*, who is 5 feet, 6 1/2 inches.

Players from Liverpool, *in red*, and Manchester City, *in blue*, compete for a header during a 2017 match.

While teams everywhere used this style, it became most associated with English soccer. One of the reasons it was so popular was because during the 1960s and 1970s, teams didn't always play on perfect fields. Even in big stadiums, the rainy English weather turned the field into a mud pit. It was nearly impossible to move the ball with short, quick passes. As field care became more of a science, teams were able to change their style of play.

THE CRAZY GANG

One of the most famous long-ball teams England ever saw was Wimbledon in 1987–88. The team was filled with tough, physical players who didn't have much skill. The media dubbed the team the "Crazy Gang" for their rough play. But Wimbledon reached the FA Cup final, a knockout style tournament in England. It was a heavy underdog against Liverpool, a team filled with superstars. But Wimbledon won the match 1–0 on a headed goal by midfielder Lawrie Sanchez.

However, the long ball still had a place in England. The country had always favored physical soccer, which meant having big forwards who could get close to the goal and smash home headers. Every English club seemed to have one.

LEVELING THE PLAYING FIELD

The English Premier League was created in 1992. It quickly became one of the best and richest leagues in the world. Its top teams, such as Manchester United, Chelsea, Liverpool, and later Manchester City, could afford to go out and sign the top players in the world. Over time, the talent on those teams allowed them to evolve and play more possession-style soccer.

However, the league has 20 teams. Many of them come from smaller cities in England where they do not have as many resources. This means their rosters are usually filled with less expensive, and typically less talented, players.

One such club is Burnley. When Burnley first earned promotion to the Premier League in 2009, the city had only about 73,000 people. Its stadium, Turf Moor, holds around 22,000 fans. That made it one of the smallest grounds in the league at the time.

Like many small teams, Burnley was promoted and relegated a few times over the next handful of years. Manager Sean Dyche led the team known as the Clarets back to the Premier League in 2016. Dyche knew his team needed to play carefully to survive against bigger teams. And Burnley would have to pick its spots to attack. Direct, long-ball soccer would work. He just needed a big forward.

THE TARGET MAN

Before the 2017–18 season, Dyche signed forward Chris Wood. Wood wasn't a superstar, but he was an international-level player in his native New Zealand. He was also 6 feet, 3 inches tall and strong. He was just what Burnley needed.

The following season, Burnley played very defensively. The club rarely had the ball. Teams that play attacking, possession

Burnley manager Sean Dyche directs his team during a 2022 match.

soccer tend to play a lot of through balls. In 38 Premier League matches in 2017–18, Burnley played only 19 through balls. That was by far the fewest in the league.

Instead, when Burnley got the ball in its own end, the strategy was to kick a long, clearing ball to midfield. That's where a player like Wood came in. He was known as a "target man." That means he's a striker who has the size to win a long ball from a defender. Once he's done that, he uses his strength to hold possession until his teammates can catch up and join the attack.

If Wood could hold the ball long enough, he could get a pass to a winger. From there he could try to find his way into the penalty area. If Wood or another striker could get open, Burnley's wingers could find them with crosses for close-range headers or shots.

Not everyone liked watching Burnley play. The Clarets didn't take many shots. Opposing fans sometimes chanted "boring, boring, Burnley" at them. Soccer commentators called Dyche's tactics old-fashioned.

However, it worked for the small club. Wood led Burnley with 10 goals in 2017–18. Burnley shocked the Premier League by finishing the year in seventh place. That spot earned the club entry into the next season's Europa League, which is a European competition for teams that miss out on the Champions League. Burnley had not played in a European competition since 1967. It was a major feat for a team that was one of the poorest clubs ever to play in the Premier League.

Burnley forward Chris Wood celebrates scoring a goal during a 2018 match against West Ham United.

GLOSSARY

cross

A pass delivered from the side of the field toward the middle.

formations

The general way teams position their players on the field.

leg

One of two matches in a series.

manager

Another name for a soccer team's head coach.

penalty area

The box in front of the goal where a player is granted a penalty kick if he or she is fouled.

promoted

When a team moves up from a lower level of competition to a higher league.

relegated

When a team is demoted from a higher league to a lower league.

rival

An opponent with whom a player or team has a fierce and ongoing competition.

stoppage time

Also known as injury time, a number of minutes tacked on to the end of a half for stoppages that occurred during play because of injuries, free kicks, and goals.

striker

A player whose primary responsibility is to create scoring chances and score goals.

through ball

A pass between defenders to an open space where a teammate will soon be.

veteran

A person who has many years of experience in a certain field.

MORE INFORMATION

Books

Donnelly, Patrick. *The Best Managers of World Soccer.* Minneapolis, MN: Abdo Publishing, 2024.

Hewson, Anthony K. *GOATs of Soccer.* Minneapolis, MN: Abdo Publishing, 2022.

Marthaler, Jon. *The Best Teams of World Soccer.* Minneapolis, MN: Abdo Publishing, 2024.

Online Resources

To learn more about soccer strategies, please visit **abdobooklinks.com** or scan this QR code. These links are routinely monitored and updated to provide the most current information available.

INDEX

About the Author

David J. Clarke is a freelance sportswriter. Originally from Helena, Montana, he now lives in Savannah, Georgia, with his golden retriever, Gus.